I0706639

To:

je t'aime

je t'aime

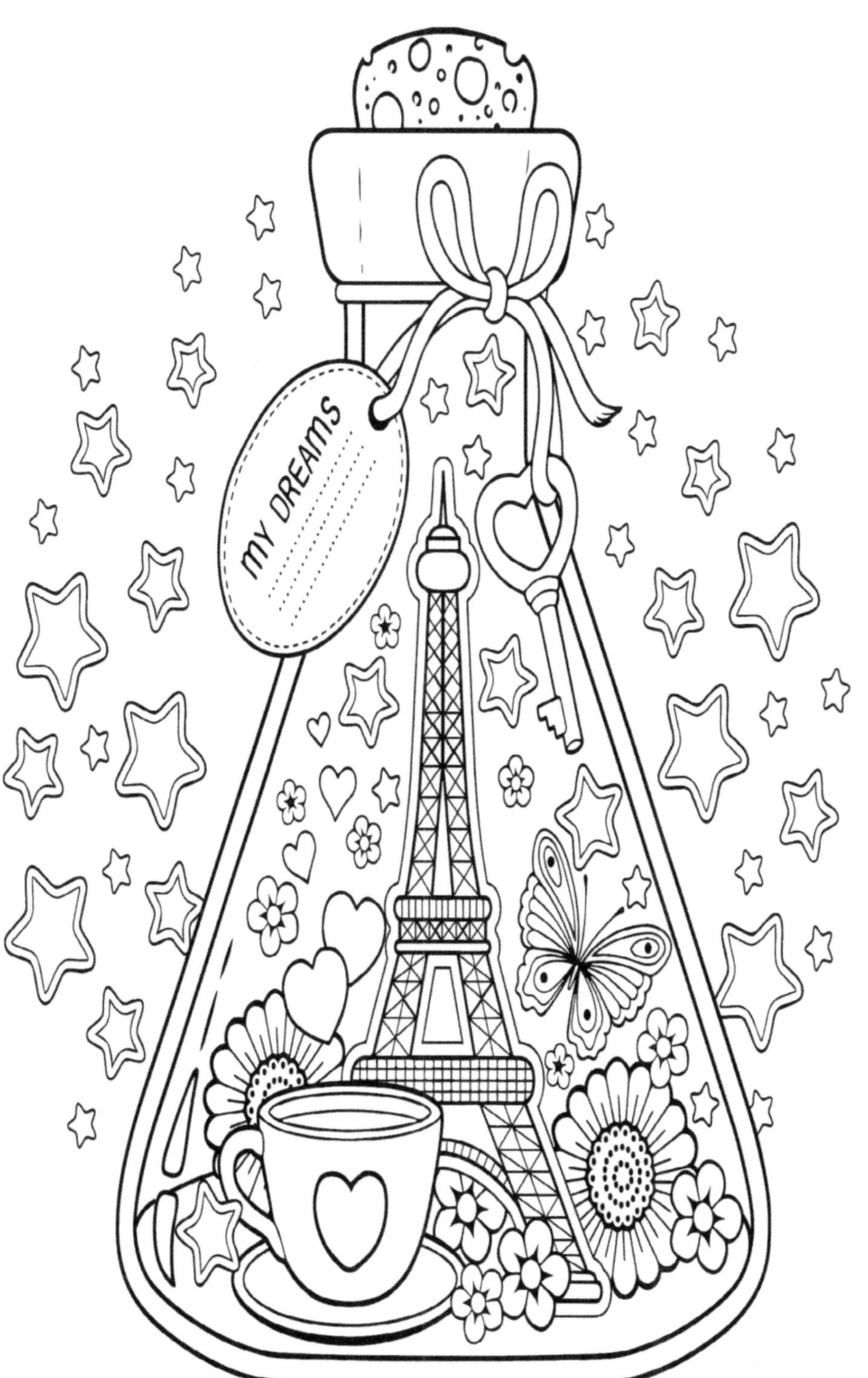
MY DREAMS

XOXO

Я люблю тебя

you are
my
sunshine

Mon Amour

For you

you are
the
best

you are
loved

Ti amo

Be Mine

I love
YOU
to the
moon
AND
back

Love

Ich liebe dich

I love you
more
than all
stars
in the sky

To My Amazing
Sister
Happy Valentine's
Day!
Coloring
Card

AFGREKI
EU TE AMO
Aishiteru
MILUJI TĚ
T'estimo Je t'aime
Te dua VOLIM TE
Ľúbim t'a
Te ubesk
Kocham Ciebie
I love you
Ti amo
S'agapo
Mi amas viN Bahibak
Ich liebe dich
M'bi fe

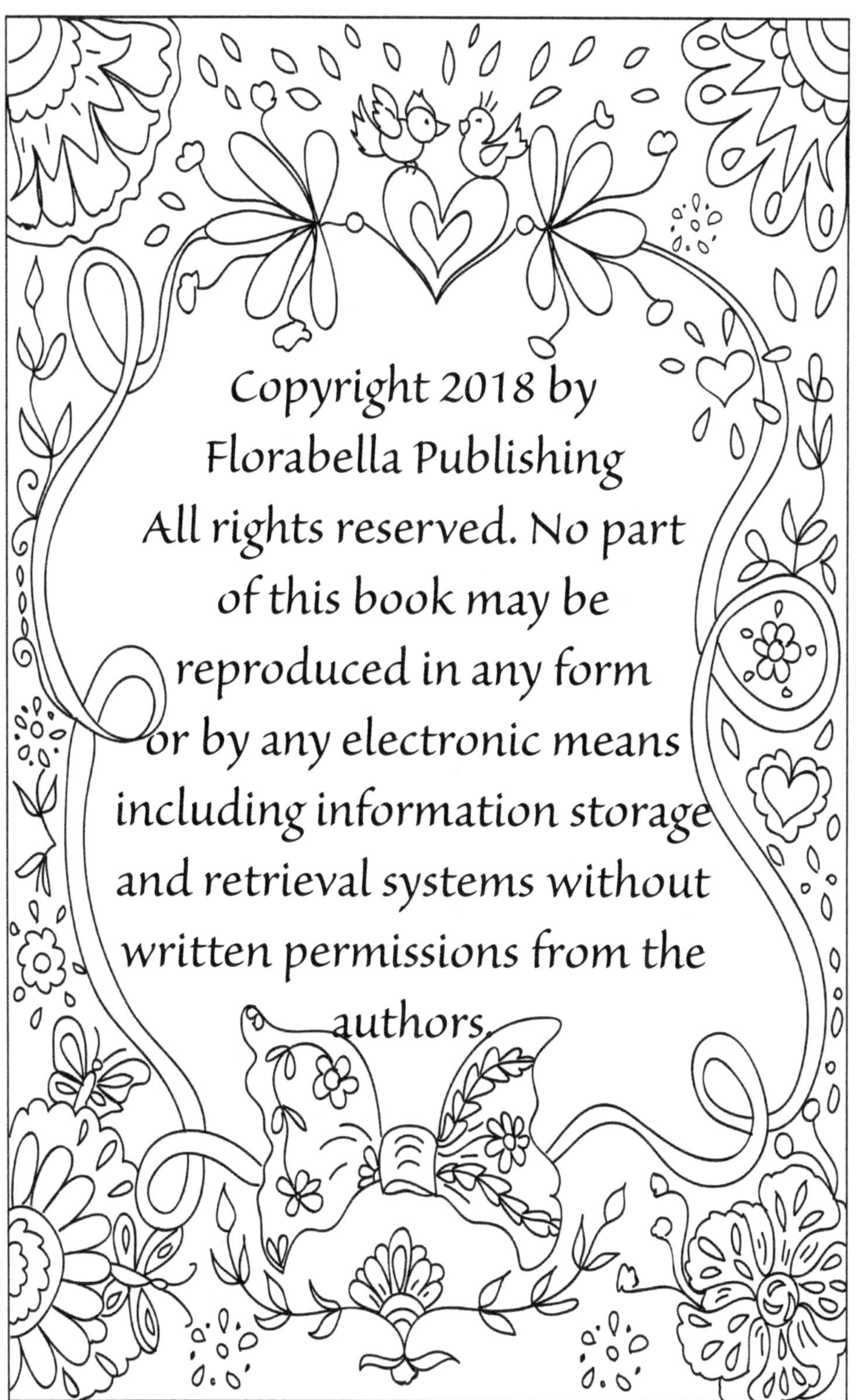
Copyright 2018 by
Florabella Publishing
All rights reserved. No part
of this book may be
reproduced in any form
or by any electronic means
including information storage
and retrieval systems without
written permissions from the
authors.

LOVE
From,